GHENT
Travel Guide 2024

Discover Ghent's Timeless Charms: A Journey through History, Culture, and Culinary Delights in the Heart of Belgium

Betty Vanslyke

Copyright © 2024 by Betty Vanslyke

All rights reserved. No part of this publication may be reproduced, distributed, or transmitted in any form or by any means, including photocopying, recording, or other electronic or mechanical methods, without the prior written permission of the publisher, except in the case of brief quotations embodied in critical reviews and certain other noncommercial uses permitted by copyright law.

TABLE OF CONTENT

TABLE OF CONTENT _____ 2

MAP OF GHENT _____ 5

INTRODUCTION _____ 6

Overview of Ghent _____ 7

Brief History and Significance _____ 9

CHAPTER ONE _____ 12

Getting to Ghent _____ 12

Transportation Options _____ 14

Getting Around Ghent _____ 15

Airport Information _____ 16

Public Transportation within the City _____ 18

CHAPTER TWO _____ 22

Accommodation Options in Ghent _____ 22

Hotels, hostels, and boutique options _____ 22

Neighborhood Recommendations _____ 30

CHAPTER THREE _____ 34

Exploring Ghent _____ 34

Must-Visit Landmarks and Attractions _____ 34

Hidden Gems and Local Favorites _____ 37

GHENT

CHAPTER FOUR 41

Cultural Experiences 41

Museums and Art Galleries 41

Theatres and Cultural Events 44

CHAPTER FIVE 48

Culinary Delights 48

Local Cuisine and Specialties 48

Popular Restaurants and Cafés 51

CHAPTER SIX 58

Nightlife 58

Bars, Pubs, and Clubs 58

Evening Entertainment Options 61

CHAPTER SEVEN 65

Shopping 65

Unique Boutiques and Markets 65

Souvenirs and Local Products in Ghent 68

CHAPTER EIGHT 72

Outdoor Activities 72

Parks and Gardens 72

CHAPTER NINE 79

Day Trips 79

Nearby Attractions and Excursions from Ghent 79

Ghent Travel Guide 2024   Page 3

GHENT

CHAPTER TEN 83

Practical Information 83

Currency, language, and useful phrases 83

Safety Tips 84

CHAPTER ELEVEN 88

Seasonal Guide 88

Best Times to Visit Ghent: 88

Festivals and Events throughout the Year: 90

CHAPTER TWELVE 94

Photography Spots 94

Scenic Locations for Memorable Moments in Ghent: 94

CHAPTER THIRTEEN 98

Local Tips and Etiquette 98

Cultural Norms and Etiquette for Visitors 98

CONCLUSION 102

Your Ghent Adventure Awaits! 102

Ghent Travel Guide 2024   Page 4

MAP OF GHENT

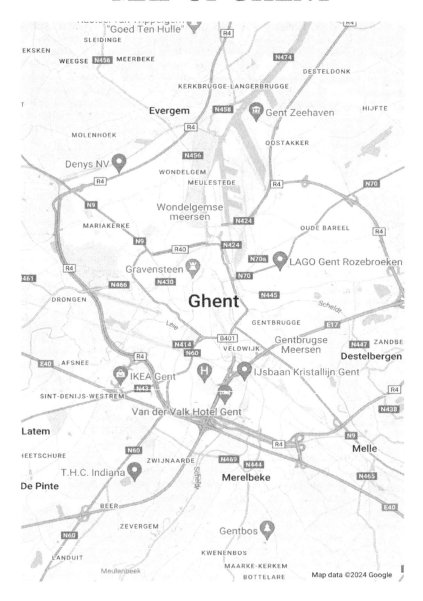

Aerial view of Ghent

INTRODUCTION

Overview of Ghent

Nestled in the heart of Belgium, Ghent is a captivating city that seamlessly blends medieval charm with a vibrant contemporary atmosphere. As you embark on your

journey through Ghent, you'll find yourself enchanted by its picturesque canals, historic architecture, and a rich cultural tapestry that spans centuries.

Medieval Marvel:

Ghent's medieval roots are evident in its well-preserved architecture, including the iconic Gravensteen Castle. The city's skyline is adorned with spires and turrets that tell tales of a bygone era, inviting you to step back in time as you wander through cobblestone streets.

Cultural Gem:

Beyond its medieval allure, Ghent is a thriving cultural hub. Home to world-class museums, art galleries, and theaters, the city embraces both tradition and innovation. From the masterpieces housed in the Museum of Fine Arts to contemporary performances at the Vooruit Arts Centre, Ghent offers a diverse cultural experience.

Canals and Waterways:

Ghent's scenic canals add a touch of romance to the cityscape. Take a leisurely boat ride to appreciate the architecture from a different perspective, or simply stroll along the water's edge, discovering charming bridges and hidden corners that make Ghent a photographer's paradise.

Gastronomic Delights:

Indulge your taste buds in Ghent's culinary scene, where Belgian specialties and international influences converge. From hearty Flemish stews to delectable chocolates, the city's eateries and markets are a culinary adventure waiting to be explored.

Dynamic Atmosphere:

While history whispers through the medieval alleys, Ghent is a dynamic city with a youthful spirit. The presence of Ghent University infuses the streets with energy, creating a lively blend of tradition and modernity.

As you embark on your Ghent adventure, this overview is just the beginning of the tapestry that awaits you. Discover the magic of Ghent, where every cobblestone has a story to tell and every canal reflects the city's timeless allure.

Brief History and Significance

Historical Tapestry:

Ghent's history is a tapestry woven with threads of resilience, prosperity, and cultural richness. Dating back to the Roman era, Ghent evolved into a prominent medieval city during the Middle Ages. Its strategic location at the confluence of rivers made it a thriving trading hub, fostering economic growth and cultural exchange.

Medieval Splendor:

During the Middle Ages, Ghent emerged as one of Europe's largest and wealthiest cities. The construction of awe-inspiring landmarks, such as the Belfry of Ghent and Saint Bavo's Cathedral, showcased the city's architectural prowess. The powerful guilds and merchants contributed to the flourishing arts and crafts that define Ghent's medieval splendor.

The Ghent Altarpiece:

Ghent's artistic legacy reached its pinnacle with the creation of the Ghent Altarpiece, a masterpiece by the Van Eyck brothers. This renowned polyptych, housed in Saint Bavo's Cathedral, is a testament to the city's patronage of the arts during the Northern Renaissance.

Challenges and Triumphs:

Ghent faced challenges over the centuries, including political unrest and economic fluctuations. The city's struggles during the industrial revolution and the World Wars shaped its resilience and determination to preserve its cultural heritage.

Modern Renaissance:

In the contemporary era, Ghent has experienced a renaissance, embracing a progressive spirit while preserving its historical identity. The presence of Ghent University has infused the city with intellectual vigor, making it a dynamic center for education and innovation.

Global Impact:

Ghent's significance extends beyond its borders. Its role in medieval trade, cultural contributions, and historical landmarks have left an indelible mark on European history. Today, as a UNESCO World Heritage Site, Ghent stands as a living testament to the harmonious coexistence of past and present.

Explore the layers of history within Ghent's cobblestone streets, where each building and artifact echoes the city's remarkable journey through time. From medieval grandeur to contemporary dynamism, Ghent's history is an integral part of its enduring allure.

CHAPTER ONE

Getting to Ghent

The Unexpected Ride with a Local Ghent Artist

On a solo trip in Ghent, Belgium, and I was trying to figure out how to get to the Gravensteen Castle. I had been walking for a while and I was starting to get tired, so I decided to take the tram.

The tram was crowded, and I was standing in the aisle. I was looking out the window when I noticed a man sitting across from me who was sketching in a notebook. He had a long beard and a beret, and he looked like a stereotypical artist.

I decided to strike up a conversation with him. I asked him what he was sketching, and he told me that he was drawing the view from the tram. He said that he loved to take the tram because it gave him a chance to see the city from a different perspective.

We talked for a while about the city, and I told him that I was a tourist from America. He was surprised to hear that I had come all the way to Ghent from America, and he asked me why I had chosen his city.

GHENT

I told him that I had always been interested in European history, and that Ghent had a fascinating history. I also told him that I had heard that Ghent was a beautiful city, and that I wanted to see it for myself.

He was pleased to hear that I liked Ghent, and he offered to show me around the city. I was hesitant at first, but I eventually agreed.

We got off the tram at the next stop, and he introduced himself as Piet. He was a painter, and he had a studio in the Patershol district.

He showed me around the studio, and I was impressed by his work. He painted landscapes and portraits, and his work was full of color and life.

He then took me on a walking tour of the city. We saw all the major sights, including the Graslei and Korenlei, the Ghent Belfry, and the Saint Nicholas' Church.

We also went to some of the lesser-known attractions, such as the Museum of Industrial Archaeology and the Castle of Gerard the Devil.

I had a wonderful time with Piet, and I learned a lot about Ghent from him. He was a kind and generous host, and I was grateful for his hospitality.

Ghent Travel Guide 2024

The unexpected ride with the local artist was one of the highlights of my trip to Ghent. It was a reminder that the best things in life often happen when you least expect them.

Transportation Options

Arriving in Ghent:

Ghent is conveniently accessible by various means of transportation, ensuring a smooth arrival for travelers.

1. **By Air**:

- *Brussels Airport (BRU)*: Located approximately 45 minutes away, Brussels Airport is a major international gateway. From here, you can easily reach Ghent by train or taxi.

- *Brussels South Charleroi Airport (CRL)*: Another option, Charleroi Airport is about a 90-minute drive from Ghent, with shuttle services and taxis available for the journey.

2. **By Train**:

- Ghent boasts excellent rail connections. The Ghent-Saint-Pieters railway station is a major hub, providing high-speed and regional train services.

The city is well-connected to major Belgian cities and neighboring countries.

3. **By Car**:

- If you prefer a road trip, Ghent is easily accessible by car. The city is well-connected to the European road network, and parking facilities are available throughout the city.

Getting Around Ghent

Once in Ghent, exploring the city is a delight with various transportation options at your disposal.

1. **Public Transport**:

- Ghent's efficient public transport system includes buses and trams. The De Lijn network covers the city and its surroundings, offering a convenient way to navigate.

2. **Bicycles**:

- Embrace the city's bike-friendly culture by renting a bicycle. Ghent boasts dedicated cycling lanes and bike-sharing programs, providing an eco-friendly and leisurely way to explore.

3. **Walking**:

- Ghent's compact city center invites exploration on foot. Wander through medieval streets, along canals, and discover hidden gems at your own pace.

4. **Taxis and Rideshares**:

- Taxis are readily available in Ghent, offering a convenient option for reaching specific destinations. Rideshare services also operate in the city.

Navigating Ghent is a seamless experience, whether you prefer the speed of trains, the flexibility of cars, or the charm of exploring on foot or by bicycle. Choose the mode of transportation that suits your preferences, and embark on a memorable journey through this enchanting city.

Airport Information

Brussels Airport (BRU):

Location:

Brussels Airport, also known as Zaventem Airport, is located approximately 45 kilometers northeast of Ghent.

Transportation to Ghent:

- **Train**: Direct train services connect Brussels Airport to Ghent. The journey takes around 1 hour, and trains depart regularly from the airport's railway station.

- **Taxi**: Taxis are readily available at the airport. The journey to Ghent by taxi takes about 45 minutes, depending on traffic conditions.

Facilities:

- Brussels Airport offers a range of amenities, including shopping outlets, restaurants, lounges, and duty-free stores.

- Currency exchange services and ATMs are available for financial transactions.

- Free Wi-Fi is accessible throughout the airport.

Brussels South Charleroi Airport (CRL):

Location:

Charleroi Airport is located approximately 90 kilometers south of Ghent.

Transportation to Ghent:

- **Shuttle Services**: Shuttle services connect Charleroi Airport to Ghent, providing a convenient transfer option.

- **Taxi**: Taxis are available at the airport, offering a direct route to Ghent.

Facilities:

- Charleroi Airport features facilities such as dining options, duty-free shops, and lounges.

- Currency exchange services and ATMs are available for financial transactions.

- Wi-Fi services are provided for travelers.

Navigating either of these airports is straightforward, and they serve as gateways to your Ghent adventure, offering a smooth transition into the cultural and historical richness of the city.

Public Transportation within the City

Ghent offers a well-organized public transportation system, providing convenient and efficient options for exploring the city and its surroundings.

1. **Buses and Trams (De Lijn)**:

- Ghent's public transportation network is primarily operated by De Lijn. Buses and trams cover the city and its suburbs, making it easy to reach various neighborhoods and attractions.

- Bus stops and tram stations are strategically located throughout the city, offering a comprehensive and accessible network.

2. **Ghent CityCard**:

- Consider purchasing the Ghent CityCard, which provides unlimited access to De Lijn buses and trams within the city. The card also grants admission to numerous museums and attractions, offering a cost-effective and convenient way to explore.

3. **Ghent by Foot**:

- Given Ghent's compact city center, exploring on foot is a popular and enjoyable option. Many of the main attractions, shops, and restaurants are within walking distance of each other

4. **Bicycles**:

- Embrace the local culture by renting a bicycle. Ghent is renowned for its bike-friendly infrastructure, with dedicated cycling lanes and bike-sharing programs making it easy to pedal around the city.

5. **Water Tram**:

- Experience Ghent from a unique perspective by taking the water tram. This boat service navigates the city's waterways, providing a scenic and leisurely mode of transportation.

6. **Mobility as a Service (MaaS)**:

- Ghent promotes integrated mobility solutions through MaaS. This platform allows travelers to plan, book, and pay for various modes of transportation, including public transit, taxis, and bike rentals, all through a single app.

7. **Single Tickets and Multi-Day Passes**:

- De Lijn offers various ticket options, including single-journey tickets and multi-day passes. These can be purchased at stations, on trams, or through mobile apps for added convenience.

Navigating Ghent with its public transportation system is not only practical but also provides an opportunity to immerse yourself in the local lifestyle. Whether by bus, tram, or boat, these options ensure a seamless and enjoyable journey through the charming streets of Ghent.

Gravensteen Castle

CHAPTER TWO

Accommodation Options in Ghent

Hotels, hostels, and boutique options

Ghent offers a diverse range of accommodation options, catering to different preferences and budgets. Whether you seek the historic charm of boutique hotels, the sociable atmosphere of hostels, or the comfort of well-appointed hotels, Ghent has something for every traveler.

1. **Historic Elegance**:

Hotel Harmony

- **Address**: Kraanlei 37, Ghent 9000 Belgium
- **Average price per nigh**t: $154
- **Property amenities**: Electric vehicle charging station, Free High Speed Internet (WiFi), Pool, Bar / lounge, Taxi service, Meeting rooms, 24-hour security, Baggage storage
- **Room features**: Allergy-free room, Soundproof rooms, Air conditioning, Private balcony, Room service, Minibar, Flatscreen TV, Complimentary toiletries

GHENT

- **Room types**: Bridal suite, Non-smoking rooms, Suites, Family rooms
- **Good to know**: HOTEL CLASS (4 Star), HOTEL STYLE (Great View, Romantic)
- **Languages spoken**: English, French, Dutch, German

Embrace the historic ambiance of Hotel Harmony, located near the Gravensteen Castle. This boutique hotel combines classic charm with modern amenities, offering a tranquil retreat in the heart of the city.

1898 The Post

- **Address**: Graslei 16, Ghent 9000 Belgium
- **Average price per night**: $171
- **Property amenities**: Paid private parking nearby, Free High Speed Internet (WiFi), Bar / lounge, Bicycle rental, Board games / puzzles, Meeting rooms, 24-hour security, Baggage storage

- **Room features**: Soundproof rooms, Bathrobes, Air conditioning, Housekeeping, Room service, Coffee / tea maker, Flatscreen TV, Bath / shower
- **Room types**: Non-smoking rooms, Suites, Family rooms,
- **Good to know**: HOTEL STYLE (Romantic, Quirky Hotels)
- **Languages Spoken**: English, French, Spanish, Dutch

Housed in a former post office building, 1898 The Post is a unique boutique hotel with individually designed rooms. The central location provides easy access to Ghent's main attractions.

2. **Modern Comfort**:

Pillows Grand Boutique Hotel Reylof Ghent

- **Address**: Hoogstraat 36, Ghent 9000 Belgium
- **Average price per night**: $175
- **Property amenities**: Electric vehicle charging station, Free High Speed Internet (WiFi), Indoor

pool, Fitness Center with Gym / Workout Room, Bar / lounge, Bicycle rental, Conference facilities, Banquet room

- **Room features**: Soundproof rooms, Air conditioning, Housekeeping, Private balcony, Room service, Minibar, Refrigerator, Flatscreen TV
- **Room types**: Bridal suite, Non-smoking rooms, Suites, Family rooms
- **Good to know**: HOTEL CLASS (4 star), HOTEL STYLE (Green, Romantic)
- **Languages spoken**: English, French, Dutch, German

Experience contemporary luxury at Pillows Grand Boutique Hotel Reylof Ghent. Stylish rooms, a spa, and a rooftop bar contribute to an upscale stay in the city center.

Ghent Marriott Hotel

- **Address**: Korenlei 10, Ghent 9000 Belgium
- **Phone**: 009 1 844-631-0595
- **Average price per night**: $166
- **Property amenities**: Paid private parking on-site, Free internet, Fitness Center with Gym / Workout Room, Bar / lounge, Bicycle rental,

Boating, Children's television networks, Highchairs available

- **Room features**: Allergy-free room, Blackout curtains, Air conditioning, Desk, Housekeeping, Coffee / tea maker, Cable / satellite TV, Bath / shower
- **Room types**: City view, Landmark view, Bridal suite, Non-smoking rooms, Suites, Family rooms
- **Good to know**: HOTEL CLASS (4 Star), HOTEL STYLE (Green, Modern)
- **Languages spoken**: English, French, Spanish, Dutch

Located along the banks of the River Lys, Ghent Marriott Hotel offers modern comfort with scenic views. The hotel's central location is ideal for exploring Ghent's landmarks.

3. **Budget-Friendly and Social**:

Hostel Uppelink

- **Address**: Sint-Michielsplein 21 Next to the bridge, Ghent 9000 Belgium
- **Average price per night**: $NA

- **Property amenities**: Paid public parking nearby, Free High Speed Internet (WiFi), Bar / lounge, Canoeing, Baggage storage, Concierge, Express check-in / check-out, Private check-in / check-out
- **Room features**: Safe
- **Room types**: Non-smoking rooms
- **Good to know**: HOTEL STYLE (Great View, Budget)
- **Languages spoken**: English, French, Dutch

For budget-conscious travelers, Hostel Uppelink offers a friendly atmosphere in a historic building near Graslei. Dormitory and private rooms are available.

Hostel 47

- **Address**: Blekerijstraat 47, Ghent 9000 Belgium
- **Average price per night**: $NA
- **Property amenities**: Paid public parking nearby, Free High Speed Internet (WiFi), Board games / puzzles, Children's television networks, Pets Allowed (Dog / Pet Friendly), Non-smoking hotel, Shared bathroom, Private check-in / check-out
- **Room features**: Safe
- **Room types**: Non-smoking rooms, Family rooms

- **Good to know**: HOTEL STYLE (Budget, Modern)
- **Languages spoken**: English, French, Dutch, German

Situated in the lively Patershol district, Hostel 47 provides a vibrant hostel experience with shared facilities and a communal kitchen. The hostel's social spaces make it easy to connect with fellow travelers.

4. **Charming Guesthouses**:

Charme Hotel Hancelot

- **Address**: Vijfwindgatenstraat 19, Ghent 9000 Belgium
- **Average price per nigh**t: $88
- **Property amenities**: Paid private parking on-site, Free High Speed Internet (WiFi), Breakfast buffet, Meeting rooms, Baggage storage, Non-smoking hotel, Express check-in / check-out, Private check-in / check-out
- **Room features**: Safe, VIP room facilities, Flatscreen TV, Bath / shower, Hair dryer
- **Room types**: Bridal suite, Non-smoking rooms, Suites

- **Good to know**: HOTEL STYLE (Historic Hotel, Residential Neighborhood)
- **Languages spoken**: English, French, Russian, Spanish, Dutch

Housed in a 17th-century mansion, Charme Hotel Hancelot offers an intimate and charming stay. The personalized service and elegant decor create a home-away-from-home atmosphere.

13 O'Clock Hostel Ghent

- **Address**: Universiteitstraat 13, Ghent 9000 Belgium
- **Average price per night**: $NA

Combining the charm of a guesthouse with the affordability of a hostel, 13 O'Clock Hostel Ghent provides a cozy and welcoming environment for travelers.

Explore Ghent's neighborhoods to discover the perfect accommodation that complements your travel style, whether it's a historic hotel, a modern retreat, or a budget-friendly hostel.

Neighborhood Recommendations

Ghent is a city with diverse neighborhoods, each offering a unique atmosphere and a distinct blend of history, culture, and modernity. Here are some neighborhood recommendations to help you find the ideal spot for your stay:

1. *Historic Center*:

- *Overview*: The heart of Ghent, the Historic Center, is characterized by medieval architecture, cobblestone streets, and picturesque canals.

- *Attractions*: Gravensteen Castle, Saint Bavo's Cathedral, and the Belfry of Ghent.

- *Accommodation*: Boutique hotels and charming guesthouses provide an authentic experience amid historic landmarks.

2. **Patershol**:

- *Overview*: Known for its narrow alleys and historic charm, Patershol is a quaint neighborhood with a bohemian atmosphere.

- *Attractions*: Patershol is home to a variety of restaurants, cafes, and local shops.

- *Accommodation*: Charming guesthouses and budget-friendly options make Patershol a cozy choice.

3. **Kouter**:

- *Overview*: Kouter is an elegant neighborhood featuring tree-lined streets, upscale boutiques, and cultural venues.

- *Attractions*: Kouter hosts the Flower Market and is close to cultural institutions like the Opera and Concert Hall.

- *Accommodation*: Upscale hotels offer a luxurious stay with easy access to cultural events.

4. **Stationsbuurt-Noord**:

- *Overview*: The area around Ghent's main railway station, Stationsbuurt-Noord, is a hub of activity with modern amenities.

- *Attractions*: Proximity to the railway station makes it convenient for travelers, and there are shopping and dining options nearby.

- *Accommodation*: Hotels catering to various budgets, making it suitable for business and leisure travelers.

5. **Korenmarkt**:

- *Overview*: Korenmarkt is a lively square surrounded by historic buildings, cafes, and shops.

- *Attractions*: The square is a central meeting point and often hosts events and festivals.

- *Accommodation*: Nearby hotels provide easy access to the vibrant atmosphere of Korenmarkt.

6. **South District (Zuid)**:

- OveIrview: The South District is known for its art scene, trendy shops, and modern architecture.

- *Attractions*: The Museum of Fine Arts and the Citadelpark are highlights of this district.

- *Accommodation*: Stylish hotels and guesthouses cater to those seeking a contemporary and cultural experience.

Consider your preferences, whether it's the historic charm of the city center, the bohemian vibes of Patershol, or the modern allure of the South District. Each neighborhood in Ghent offers a unique experience, ensuring a memorable stay in this enchanting city.

Saint Bavo's Cathedral

CHAPTER THREE

Exploring Ghent

Must-Visit Landmarks and Attractions

Ghent is a city rich in history and culture, boasting a plethora of landmarks and attractions that captivate visitors. Here are some must-visit places that showcase the essence of Ghent:

1. Gravensteen Castle:

- *Overview*: Step back in time at Gravensteen Castle, a medieval fortress in the heart of Ghent. Explore the castle's dungeons, towers, and ramparts while enjoying panoramic views of the city.

2. Saint Bavo's Cathedral:

- *Overview*: Saint Bavo's Cathedral is a masterpiece of Gothic architecture, known for housing the Ghent Altarpiece by the Van Eyck brothers. Marvel at the stunning stained glass windows and intricate details of this iconic cathedral.

3. **Belfry of Ghent**:

- *Overview*: Climb the Belfry of Ghent for a panoramic view of the city. This medieval bell tower, part of the UNESCO World Heritage Site, offers a unique perspective of Ghent's skyline.

4. **Graslei and Korenlei**:

- *Overview*: These picturesque quays along the river Lys are lined with historic guild houses. Graslei and Korenlei form one of the most scenic spots in Ghent, perfect for a leisurely stroll and photos.

5. **St. Michael's Bridge**:

- *Overview*: St. Michael's Bridge offers a stunning vantage point for capturing Ghent's skyline. Enjoy views of Graslei, Korenlei, and the medieval architecture that defines the city.

6. **Ghent Altarpiece (Adoration of the Mystic Lamb)**:

- *Overview*: Visit Saint Bavo's Cathedral to see the Ghent Altarpiece, a masterpiece of Northern Renaissance art. Admire the intricate details and symbolism in this renowned polyptych.

7. **Gentse Floraliënhal (Flower Market)**:

- **Overview**: The Flower Market on Kouter is a vibrant display of colors and fragrances. If you visit in spring, you'll witness a stunning array of flowers and plants in this lively market.

8. **STAM Ghent City Museum**:

- *Overview*: Delve into Ghent's history at the STAM Ghent City Museum. Interactive exhibits and multimedia displays provide insights into the city's evolution from medieval times to the present.

9. **Vrijdagmarkt**:

- *Overview*: Vrijdagmarkt, the Friday Market, is one of the oldest squares in Ghent. Surrounded by cafes and historic buildings, it's a great place to experience local life and enjoy outdoor dining.

10. **Citadelpark**:

- *Overview*: Escape to the tranquility of Citadelpark, a green oasis in the city. This park features walking paths, sculptures, and the Museum of Fine Arts, offering a peaceful retreat.

These landmarks and attractions weave together the historical, cultural, and artistic tapestry of Ghent. Each visit promises a journey through time and a deeper appreciation for the city's unique charm.

Hidden Gems and Local Favorites

Discovering the hidden gems and local favorites in Ghent allows you to experience the city beyond the well-known landmarks. Here are some lesser-known treasures and beloved spots cherished by locals:

1. **Patershol**:

- **Overview**: Tucked away near Gravensteen Castle, Patershol is a charming neighborhood with narrow cobblestone streets, historic houses, and a bohemian atmosphere. Explore its hidden corners and discover local eateries and boutique shops.

2. **The Werregarenstraat Alley (Graffiti Street)**:

- *Overview*: Immerse yourself in vibrant street art at Werregarenstraat, known as Ghent's Graffiti Street. The ever-changing murals and graffiti create a dynamic outdoor art gallery.

GHENT

3. **Café Afsnis**:

- Overview: Café Afsnis is a cozy and eclectic spot favored by locals. Enjoy live music, poetry readings, and a laid-back atmosphere. It's an ideal place to experience Ghent's vibrant arts scene.

4. **Baudelopark**:

- *Overview*: Baudelopark offers a peaceful escape from the bustling city. This green oasis features ponds, walking paths, and sculptures, providing a serene environment for relaxation.

5. **Keizerpark**:

- *Overview*: Keizerpark is a hidden gem along the river Lys, offering a tranquil setting for a leisurely stroll or a picnic. Enjoy views of the water and the city skyline from this peaceful park.

6. **The Holy Food Market**:

- *Overview*: Located in a former church, The Holy Food Market is a unique culinary experience. This food hall brings together diverse cuisines, offering a delightful array of international flavors.

Ghent Travel Guide 2024

7. **The Cat Caboose**:

- *Overview*: For cat lovers, The Cat Caboose is a quirky and cozy café with resident feline companions. Enjoy a cup of coffee or tea while interacting with the friendly cats.

8. **Groot Vleeshuis**:

- *Overview*: Groot Vleeshuis, or the Great Butcher's Hall, is a hidden gem for food enthusiasts. This historic building showcases local products and traditional Flemish delicacies.

9. **The House of Alijn**:

- *Overview*: The House of Alijn is a museum that provides a glimpse into Belgian folk life. Explore the exhibits featuring everyday objects and traditions, offering a nostalgic journey through the past.

10. **Café 't Galgenhuis**:

- *Overview*: Café 't Galgenhuis is one of Ghent's smallest and oldest pubs, tucked away in a narrow alley. Its historic ambiance and extensive beer menu make it a favorite among locals.

Venture off the beaten path to discover these hidden gems and local favorites, adding a layer of authenticity to your Ghent experience. Whether it's street art, charming neighborhoods, or unique cafes, these spots offer a glimpse into the soul of the city.

CHAPTER FOUR

Cultural Experiences

Museums and Art Galleries

Ghent's cultural landscape is enriched by a variety of museums and art galleries, each offering a unique perspective on the city's history, art, and innovation. Here are some must-visit cultural institutions:

1. **Museum of Fine Arts (MSK)**:

- *Overview*: The Museum of Fine Arts is home to an impressive collection of Flemish and Belgian paintings from the Middle Ages to the 20th century. Masterpieces by artists such as Jan van Eyck and Hieronymus Bosch are showcased.

2. **Stam Ghent City Museum**:

- *Overview*: Stam Ghent City Museum explores the city's history and development through interactive exhibits and multimedia displays. It's a fascinating journey from medieval Ghent to the present day.

3. **Design Museum Gent**:

- *Overview*: Design Museum Gent celebrates design and decorative arts. The collection spans historical pieces to contemporary design, providing insights into the evolution of design over the centuries.

4. **STORY**:

- *Overview*: STORY is an interactive museum that brings the history of Ghent to life through multimedia installations and immersive experiences. It's a modern and engaging way to explore the city's past.

5. **Dr. Guislain Museum**:

- *Overview*: The Dr. Guislain Museum, located in a former psychiatric hospital, explores the history of psychiatry. It houses a unique collection of art created by psychiatric patients.

6. **The House of Alijn**:

- *Overview*: The House of Alijn is a museum that offers a nostalgic journey into Belgian folk life. The exhibits feature everyday objects and traditions, providing a charming glimpse into the past.

GHENT

7. S.M.A.K. (Stedelijk Museum voor Actuele Kunst):

- *Overview*: S.M.A.K. is Ghent's contemporary art museum, showcasing a diverse collection of modern and contemporary artworks. The museum often features temporary exhibitions by leading contemporary artists.

8. Ghent City Pavilion:

- *Overview*: The Ghent City Pavilion is an architectural gem designed by Robbrecht en Daem. It serves as an information hub and exhibition space, providing insight into the city's urban development.

9. The World of Kina:

- *Overview*: The World of Kina consists of two natural history museums, emphasizing interactive exhibits for children. It's an educational and entertaining destination for families.

10. Gallery Pinsart:

- *Overview*: Gallery Pinsart is a contemporary art gallery that features works by both established and

Ghent Travel Guide 2024   Page 43

emerging artists. It provides a platform for artistic expression in various forms.

Explore Ghent's cultural scene by visiting these museums and art galleries, where history, art, and innovation converge to create a vibrant and enriching experience for visitors.

Theatres and Cultural Events

Ghent's vibrant cultural scene is enriched by its theaters and a calendar filled with exciting cultural events. Whether you're interested in live performances, festivals, or theatrical productions, Ghent offers a diverse array of options. Here are some theaters and cultural events to consider:

1. **Vooruit Arts Centre**:

- *Overview*: Vooruit is a cultural center housed in an iconic building that hosts a variety of events, including concerts, dance performances, theater productions, and art exhibitions.

2. **Capitole Ghent**:

- *Overview*: Capitole Ghent is a historic theater known for its grandeur and hosts a range of events, from musicals and concerts to comedy shows and theatrical performances.

3. NTGent - Royal Dutch Theatre:

- *Overview*: NTGent is a renowned theater company that stages a diverse repertoire of plays, from classic dramas to contemporary works. The Royal Dutch Theatre is their main venue.

4. Ghent Festival (Gentse Feesten):

- *Overview*: The Ghent Festival, held in July, is one of Europe's largest cultural festivals. It features a vibrant mix of music, theater, street performances, and cultural activities throughout the city.

5. Ghent Film Festival (Film Fest Gent):

- *Overview*: Film Fest Gent is a prominent film festival held annually, showcasing a diverse selection of international and Belgian films. It includes screenings, premieres, and events related to the world of cinema.

GHENT

6. Gent Jazz Festival:

- *Overview*: Gent Jazz Festival is a world-class jazz festival held in July. It attracts renowned jazz musicians and provides a unique atmosphere in the historic setting of Bijloke Abbey.

7. Miramiro Circus and Street Arts Festival:

- *Overview*: Miramiro is a festival celebrating circus arts and street performances. It brings together international performers and takes place at various locations throughout the city.

8. Opera Ballet Vlaanderen - Ghent Opera House:

- *Overview*: The Ghent Opera House, part of Opera Ballet Vlaanderen, presents a diverse program of opera, ballet, and classical performances. The building itself is an architectural gem.

9. Ghent Light Festival:

- Overview: The Ghent Light Festival, held every three years, transforms the city into a mesmerizing spectacle of light installations and projections. It draws artists and spectators from around the world.

10. **KASKcinema**:

- *Overview*: KASKcinema is the cinema venue of the Royal Academy of Fine Arts. It screens a selection of independent, art-house, and experimental films, contributing to Ghent's cinematic culture.

Immerse yourself in Ghent's cultural tapestry by attending these theaters and cultural events. Whether you're a fan of live performances, film, or festivals, Ghent offers a dynamic and enriching cultural experience throughout the year.

CHAPTER FIVE

Culinary Delights

Local Cuisine and Specialties

Ghent's culinary scene is a delightful blend of traditional

Belgian flavors and innovative twists. Explore the city's gastronomic offerings by indulging in these local cuisine and specialties:

1. **Waterzooi**:

- *Overview*: A quintessential Ghent dish, Waterzooi is a hearty soup or stew made with chicken or fish, vegetables, and cream. It embodies the comfort and warmth of Belgian cuisine.

2. **Gentse Stoverij**:

- *Overview*: Gentse Stoverij is a Flemish beef stew simmered in beer, creating a rich and savory dish. It's often served with frites (Belgian fries) for a satisfying meal.

3. **Moules Frites**:

- *Overview*: While associated with Belgian coastal areas, Moules Frites (mussels with fries) is a beloved dish in Ghent too. Enjoy a pot of steamed mussels with a side of crispy fries.

4. **Belgian Waffles**:

- *Overview*: Indulge in the heavenly sweetness of Belgian waffles. Whether topped with whipped cream, chocolate sauce, or fresh fruit, Ghent offers an array of tempting waffle options.

5. **Ganda Ham**:

- *Overview*: Ganda Ham is a dry-cured ham that originates from Ghent. Delicately sliced, it makes for a delicious addition to sandwiches, salads, or as a savory snack.

6. **Cuberdon**:

- *Overview*: Known as "noses" or "Ghent noses," Cuberdons are cone-shaped candies with a sweet and fruity raspberry flavor. They are a popular treat among locals and visitors alike.

7. **Tierenteyn-Verlent Mustard**:

- *Overview*: Ghent is renowned for its exceptional mustard. Tierenteyn-Verlent is a historic mustard shop where you can purchase this flavorful condiment to add a zing to your dishes.

8. **Ghentse Neuzekes**:

- *Overview*: Ghentse Neuzekes, or Ghent noses, are cone-shaped candies with a jelly-like consistency. They come in various flavors and are a beloved sweet treat in the city.

9. **Cuberdon Jenever**:

- *Overview*: Experience the local flavors with Cuberdon Jenever, a traditional Belgian juniper-flavored spirit infused with the taste of Cuberdon candies.

10. **Gentse Mokken**:

- *Overview*: Gentse Mokken are chocolate-covered candies filled with a praline or marzipan center. They make for delightful souvenirs or sweet indulgences.

Pair these culinary delights with a Belgian beer or a locally brewed Ghent craft beer to enhance your gastronomic experience. Ghent's diverse and flavorful offerings make it a paradise for food enthusiasts.

Popular Restaurants and Cafés

Ghent boasts a vibrant culinary scene, offering a diverse range of restaurants and cafés that cater to various tastes. Here are some popular establishments where you can savor delicious dishes and experience the city's gastronomic delights:

1. **The House of Eliott**:

- *Address*: Jan Breydelstraat 36, Ghent, Flanders, Belgium, 9000
- *Website*: thehouseofeliott.be
- *Price range per person*: $23 - $46
- *Features*: Credit cards accepted, Outdoor seating, Booking
- *Overview*: A stylish restaurant located in the historic heart of Ghent, The House of Eliott offers a menu featuring Belgian and French cuisine with a modern twist. The elegant setting adds to the dining experience.

2. **'t Oud Clooster**:

- *Address*: Zwartezustersstraat 5, Ghent 9000 Belgium
- *Phone*: +32 9 233 78 02
- *Price Range*: $10 - $20
- *Cuisines*: French, Belgian, European, Gastropub
- *Special Diets*: Vegetarian Friendly, Vegan Options, Gluten Free Options
- *Meals*: Lunch, Dinner, Late Night

- *Features*: Takeout, Highchairs Available, Reservations, Outdoor Seating, Seating, Serves Alcohol, Full Bar, Accepts Mastercard, Accepts Visa, Digital Payments, Free Wifi, Accepts Credit Cards, Table Service
- *Overview*: Housed in a former cloister, 't Oud Clooster serves traditional Flemish and Belgian dishes. The atmospheric setting and outdoor terrace make it a charming spot for a relaxed meal.

3. **Dulle Griet**:

- *Address*: Vrijdagmarkt 50, 9000 Gent
- *Phone*: +32 (0)9 224 24 55
- *email*: contact@dullegriet.be
- *Opening time*
  mo: 4:30 p.m. - 1 a.m.
  tu - sa: 12 p.m. - 1 a.m.
  su: 12 p.m. - 7:30 p.m.

- *Overview*: Dulle Griet is a popular pub with an extensive beer list, including the famous Max beer. The "Max Challenge," where you need to surrender a shoe as collateral for a special beer, is a unique experience.

4. **Amadeus Ghent**:

- *Address*: Plotersgracht 8-10, Ghent 9000 Belgium
- *Phone*: +32 497 43 85 71
- *Price Range*: $13 - $22
- *Meals*: Lunch, Dinner, Late Night
- *Cuisines*: Belgian, Barbecue, European
- *Features*: Reservations, Seating, Highchairs Available, Serves Alcohol, Accepts Credit Cards, Table Service
- *Overview*: Amadeus is known for its all-you-can-eat spare ribs served with a side of Belgian fries. The casual and lively atmosphere makes it a favorite among locals and visitors alike.

5. **De Vitrine**:

- *Overview*: De Vitrine is a Michelin-starred restaurant offering a contemporary and inventive menu. Chef Kobe Desramaults showcases local and seasonal ingredients in his culinary creations.

6. **Bidon Coffee & Bicycles**:

- *Address*: Bisdomkaai 25, Ghent 9000 Belgium
- *Phone*: +32 495 24 76 97

- *Price Range*: $5 - $15
- *Cuisines*: International, European
- Meals: Breakfast, Brunch
- *Features*: Seating, Wheelchair Accessible, Full Bar, Wine and Beer, Accepts Mastercard, Accepts Visa, Digital Payments, Free Wifi, Outdoor Seating, Serves Alcohol
- *Overview*: Bidon Coffee & Bicycles is a hip café that combines a love for coffee with a passion for cycling. Enjoy specialty coffee and a cozy atmosphere surrounded by bike-themed decor.

7. **Holy Food Market**:

- *Overview*: Located in a former church, the Holy Food Market is a gastronomic paradise featuring a variety of food stalls serving international cuisine. It's a unique and vibrant culinary destination.

8. **Clouds in my Coffee**:

- *Address*: Dendermondsesteenweg 104, Ghent 9000 Belgium
- *Phone*: +32 9 336 84 34
- *Price Range*: $3 - $16
- *Cuisines*: Belgian, European

GHENT

- *Special Diets*: Vegan Options, Vegetarian Friendly
- *Features*: Reservations, Seating, Full Bar, Accepts American Express, Accepts Mastercard, Accepts Visa, Free Wifi, Table Service, Takeout, Outdoor Seating, Highchairs Available, Wheelchair Accessible, Serves Alcohol, Accepts Credit Cards
- *Overview*: Clouds in my Coffee is a trendy coffee shop that serves artisanal coffee and a selection of pastries. The modern and minimalistic interior provides a relaxed environment for coffee enthusiasts.

9. **Café de Loge**:

- *Address*: Annonciadenstraat 5, Ghent 9000 Belgium
- *Phone*: +32 9 225 34 38
- *Cuisines*: Pub, Healthy, Cafe, European
- *Special Diets*: Vegetarian Friendly, Vegan Options
- *Meals*: Lunch, Dinner, Breakfast, Brunch, Drinks
- *Features*: Reservations, Seating, Serves Alcohol
- *Overview*: Café de Loge is a laid-back café with a bohemian vibe. It hosts live music, cultural events, and offers a diverse menu of drinks and snacks.

Ghent Travel Guide 2024

10. **Bronze**:

- *Overview*: Bronze is a contemporary restaurant known for its focus on local and seasonal ingredients. The elegant setting and creative menu make it a popular choice for a refined dining experience.

Whether you're seeking traditional Belgian fare, international cuisine, or a cozy café for coffee and pastries, Ghent's culinary scene has something for every palate. Explore these popular establishments to savor the flavors of the city.

CHAPTER SIX

Nightlife

Bars, Pubs, and Clubs

Ghent comes alive in the evening with a lively and diverse nightlife scene. Whether you prefer cozy pubs, trendy bars, or vibrant clubs, Ghent has something for everyone. Here are some popular establishments to enjoy the nightlife:

1. **Hot Club de Gand**:

- *Overview*: Hot Club de Gand is a legendary jazz club in Ghent, known for its intimate atmosphere and live jazz performances. It's a must-visit for jazz enthusiasts looking for an authentic experience.

2. **Dreupelkot**:

- *Overview*: Dreupelkot is a quaint and traditional Belgian jenever bar. With a vast selection of jenevers (Belgian gin), it provides a unique and cozy setting for sampling this local spirit.

3. Trollenkelder:

- *Overview*: Nestled in the heart of Ghent, Trollenkelder is a medieval-themed bar with a vast selection of Belgian beers. The décor, featuring trolls and knights, adds a whimsical touch to the experience.

4. Café Charlatan:

- *Overview*: Café Charlatan is a popular nightlife spot with a diverse crowd. It features live music, DJ sets, and a lively dance floor, making it a great choice for a night out.

5. The Cobbler:

- *Overview*: The Cobbler is a stylish cocktail bar where skilled mixologists create unique and inventive cocktails. The cozy ambiance and expertly crafted drinks make it a favorite among cocktail enthusiasts.

6. Pauze:

- *Overview*: Pauze is a trendy wine bar with a chic and modern interior. It offers an extensive selection of wines, along with tapas and snacks, creating a sophisticated yet relaxed atmosphere.

7. **Café Bar Mirwaar**:

- *Overview*: Café Bar Mirwaar is a beloved local pub with a laid-back vibe. It's a great place to enjoy a beer, strike up a conversation with locals, and experience the friendly atmosphere.

8. **Decadance**:

- *Overview*: Decadance is a renowned club in Ghent, known for its electronic music events and vibrant dance floor. It's a favorite among those seeking an energetic and memorable night out.

9. **Dok Brewing Company**:

- *Overview*: Dok Brewing Company is a craft brewery with a spacious and modern setting. It offers a rotating selection of craft beers, making it a fantastic destination for beer enthusiasts.

10. **Vooruit Café**:

- *Overview*: Located within the Vooruit Arts Centre, Vooruit Café is a cultural hotspot that transforms into a lively bar at night. Enjoy a drink in a historic setting with occasional live performances.

Whether you're in the mood for live music, craft cocktails, or a night of dancing, Ghent's bars, pubs, and clubs provide a diverse and exciting nightlife experience.

Evening Entertainment Options

As the sun sets, Ghent transforms into a city that offers a variety of evening entertainment options. Whether you prefer cultural performances, leisurely strolls, or vibrant nightlife, Ghent has something to suit your preferences. Here are some evening entertainment options:

1. **Graslei and Korenlei by Night**:

- *Overview*: Take a leisurely evening stroll along the picturesque Graslei and Korenlei. The beautifully illuminated medieval buildings and reflections on the water create a magical atmosphere.

2. **Ghent River Cruise**:

- *Overview*: Experience Ghent from a different perspective by taking a river cruise in the evening. Enjoy the city lights reflecting on the water as you glide along the canals.

3. **Ghent Illuminated**:

- *Overview*: Ghent Illuminated is an enchanting light show that highlights the city's landmarks after dark. Various buildings are illuminated with vibrant colors, creating a captivating visual experience.

4. **Ghent Light Walk**:

- *Overview*: Join a guided Ghent Light Walk to discover the city's illuminated gems. Learn about the history of Ghent while enjoying the magical ambiance created by the evening lights.

5. **Live Performances at Vooruit Arts Centre**:

- *Overview*: Check the schedule at Vooruit Arts Centre for live performances, concerts, and cultural events. Enjoy an evening of artistic expression in this historic venue.

6. **Ghent Ghost Tour**:

- *Overview*: Embark on a Ghent Ghost Tour for a unique and entertaining evening experience. Hear captivating stories and legends as you explore the city's darker side.

Ghent Travel Guide 2024

GHENT

7. Ghent by Night Photography Tour:

- *Overview*: Join a photography tour to capture the beauty of Ghent at night. Learn tips and techniques from a professional photographer while capturing stunning nighttime shots.

8. Gastronomic Delights in Patershol:

- *Overview*: Explore the Patershol district in the evening, known for its charming cobblestone streets and diverse dining options. Enjoy a delightful dinner in one of the area's cozy restaurants.

9. Gentse Feesten (Ghent Festival):

- *Overview*: If visiting during July, experience the Ghent Festival, one of Europe's largest cultural festivals. Enjoy street performances, live music, and a festive atmosphere throughout the city.

10. Cultural Events at STAM Ghent City Museum:

- *Overview*: Check for evening cultural events at STAM Ghent City Museum. The museum often hosts lectures, exhibitions, and discussions that provide insights into Ghent's history and culture.

Ghent Travel Guide 2024

Whether you choose to explore the city's illuminated landmarks, attend a live performance, or indulge in gastronomic delights, Ghent's evening entertainment options promise a memorable and enjoyable experience.

CHAPTER SEVEN

Shopping

Unique Boutiques and Markets

Ghent is a haven for those seeking unique and locally crafted items. From boutique shops with handmade goods to vibrant markets offering a variety of treasures, here are some places where you can discover one-of-a-kind finds:

1. Ghent Flea Market (Vrijdagmarkt):

- *Overview*: Vrijdagmarkt, or the Friday Market, is one of the oldest markets in Ghent. Explore a diverse range of goods, including antiques, vintage items, and second-hand treasures. It's a perfect spot for those who love the thrill of a good find.

2. Dille & Kamille:

- *Overview*: Dille & Kamille is a charming boutique offering a curated selection of kitchenware, home goods, and gifts. With a focus on natural materials and timeless designs, it's a delightful place to explore.

GHENT

3. Chocolatier Van Hoorebeke:

- *Overview*: For a sweet and unique treat, visit Chocolatier Van Hoorebeke. This artisanal chocolate shop creates handmade chocolates using high-quality ingredients, making it an ideal spot for chocolate enthusiasts.

4. Ydee Concept Store:

- *Overview*: Ydee Concept Store is a boutique that features a carefully curated collection of fashion, accessories, and lifestyle items. Discover unique pieces created by local designers and artisans.

5. Gentse Waterzooi Shop:

- *Overview*: Gentse Waterzooi Shop celebrates the city's iconic dish, Waterzooi. Here, you can find various interpretations of Waterzooi, including ready-to-cook kits and related culinary delights.

6. Koperhuis:

- *Overview*: Koperhuis is a concept store that combines design, fashion, and interior items. Explore a carefully chosen selection of products, from stylish clothing to contemporary home decor.

Ghent Travel Guide 2024

GHENT

7. **Chocolaterie Luc Van Hoorebeke**:

- *Overview*: Another gem for chocolate lovers, Chocolaterie Luc Van Hoorebeke offers handmade chocolates with a focus on quality and craftsmanship. Indulge in exquisite pralines and chocolate creations.

8. **Côté Jardin**:

- *Overview*: Côté Jardin is a boutique garden center where you can find a variety of plants, gardening accessories, and home decor items. It's a green oasis in the heart of the city.

9. **Sofie's Lingerie**:

- *Overview*: Sofie's Lingerie is a boutique offering a personalized and expert lingerie shopping experience. Discover high-quality lingerie brands and find the perfect fit with the help of knowledgeable staff.

10. **Veldstraat**:

- *Overview*: Veldstraat is one of Ghent's main shopping streets, lined with a mix of well-known brands and unique boutiques. Explore the diverse

Ghent Travel Guide 2024 Page 67

range of shops offering fashion, accessories, and more.

Whether you're on the hunt for vintage treasures, artisanal chocolates, or unique fashion pieces, Ghent's boutiques and markets provide a delightful shopping experience with a touch of local charm.

Souvenirs and Local Products in Ghent

When exploring Ghent, be sure to bring home some distinctive souvenirs and local products that capture the essence of the city. Here are some items to consider:

1. **Ghent Cuberdons**:

- *Overview*: Ghent Cuberdons, also known as "noses," are cone-shaped candies with a jelly-like consistency and a sweet raspberry flavor. They make for a delicious and iconic Ghent souvenir.

2. **Ghent Mustard from Tierenteyn-Verlent**:

- *Overview*: Tierenteyn-Verlent is a historic mustard shop in Ghent, and their mustard is a local specialty. Bring home a jar of their flavorful mustard to add a touch of Ghent to your meals.

3. **Ganda Ham**:

- *Overview*: Ganda Ham is a dry-cured ham originating from Ghent. It's a delicious and distinctive local product that can be enjoyed on its own or as part of charcuterie.

4. **Ghent Lace**:

- *Overview*: Ghent lace is a traditional craft with a rich history. Consider purchasing lace products such as handkerchiefs, tablecloths, or intricate lace accessories as a souvenir.

5. **Belgian Chocolates**:

- *Overview*: Ghent is renowned for its Belgian chocolates. Visit local chocolatiers and select a box of handmade pralines or other chocolate delights to bring a taste of Ghent back home.

6. **Ghent Gin**:

- *Overview*: Ghent has a burgeoning craft gin scene. Look for locally produced Ghent gin with unique flavors and botanicals for a distinctive spirit to bring back as a souvenir.

7. Gentse Mokken:

- *Overview*: Gentse Mokken are chocolate-covered candies filled with praline or marzipan. These sweet treats make for delightful and portable souvenirs to share with friends and family.

8. Ghent-themed Postcards and Art Prints:

- *Overview*: Explore local art shops for Ghent-themed postcards and art prints featuring iconic landmarks, street scenes, and vibrant cityscapes. They make for affordable and artistic keepsakes.

9. Ghent Beer:

- *Overview*: Ghent boasts a rich beer culture. Select local Ghent beers, either from renowned breweries or craft beer producers, to enjoy a taste of the city's brewing heritage.

10. Local Artisanal Products:

- *Overview*: Support local artisans by exploring boutiques and markets for unique handmade items. Look for ceramics, textiles, or other crafts that showcase the talent of Ghent's creative community.

When shopping for souvenirs and local products in Ghent, consider items that resonate with your personal tastes and preferences, providing a lasting memory of your time in this charming city.

CHAPTER EIGHT

Outdoor Activities

Parks and Gardens

Ghent offers a delightful array of parks and gardens, providing tranquil spaces for relaxation, leisure, and appreciation of nature. Here are some parks and gardens to explore in the city:

1. **Citadelpark**:

- *Overview*: Citadelpark is a vast green space in the heart of Ghent. This park features walking paths, ponds, sculptures, and playgrounds. It's an ideal spot for a leisurely stroll, a picnic, or simply enjoying nature.

2. **Baudelopark**:

- *Overview*: Baudelopark is a charming urban park with a mix of greenery, ponds, and artistic installations. It offers a peaceful retreat from the bustling city and hosts occasional events.

3. **Koning Albertpark**:

- *Overview*: Koning Albertpark, located near the Ghent-Sint-Pieters railway station, is a picturesque park with a central pond, walking paths, and benches. It's a great place for a quiet break or a leisurely walk.

4. **Rooigemlaan**:

- *Overview*: Rooigemlaan is a tree-lined avenue with a pedestrian and cycling path. This scenic route is surrounded by greenery and serves as a peaceful escape for those seeking a nature-filled walk or bike ride.

5. **Stadspark**:

- *Overview*: Stadspark, or City Park, is situated near the city center and offers a green oasis with tree-lined paths and open spaces. It's a popular spot for locals to unwind and enjoy nature.

6. **Abdij van het Park (Abbey of the Park)**:

- *Overview*: While not in Ghent itself, the Abbey of the Park in Heverlee is worth a visit for its beautiful gardens. Explore the well-maintained grounds and the serene atmosphere of this historic site.

7. **Kasteel Claeys Bouüaert**:

- *Overview*: Kasteel Claeys Bouüaert is a castle surrounded by a park with lush lawns and old trees. The park is often used for cultural events and provides a peaceful setting for a leisurely stroll.

8. **Bourgoyen-Ossemeersen**:

- *Overview*: Bourgoyen-Ossemeersen is a nature reserve on the outskirts of Ghent, featuring wetlands, meadows, and walking trails. It's an excellent destination for birdwatching and nature enthusiasts.

9. **Blaisantvestpark**:

- *Overview*: Blaisantvestpark is a small urban park with a playground, green spaces, and seating areas. It offers a relaxing environment for locals and visitors to enjoy a moment of tranquility.

10. The World of Kina:

- *Overview*: The World of Kina, a natural history museum, includes a garden with a pond and native plants. It's an educational and family-friendly space where visitors can connect with nature.

Whether you're looking for a peaceful retreat, a family-friendly space, or a nature-filled walk, Ghent's parks and gardens provide diverse settings for outdoor enjoyment.

Recreational Options in Ghent

Ghent offers a variety of recreational activities for locals and visitors alike. Whether you're interested in sports, leisurely pursuits, or more active adventures, here are some recreational options to explore in the city:

1. Biking along the River Lys:

- *Overview*: Ghent is a bike-friendly city with scenic routes along the River Lys. Rent a bike and explore the picturesque landscapes and charming neighborhoods at your own pace.

Ghent Travel Guide 2024

GHENT

2. **Boat Tours on the Canals**:

- *Overview*: Experience Ghent from the water by taking a boat tour on the canals. Enjoy guided tours that provide unique perspectives of the city's landmarks and historical sites.

3. **Golf at Golf Club Ooidonk**:

- *Overview*: Golf enthusiasts can enjoy a round at Golf Club Ooidonk, located just outside Ghent. This 18-hole course is set amidst beautiful landscapes, offering a relaxing and challenging golf experience.

4. **Gentbrugse Meersen**:

- *Overview*: Gentbrugse Meersen is a large green area with walking and cycling paths, providing a natural escape within the city. It's an excellent spot for outdoor activities, picnics, and birdwatching.

5. **Ghent Skatepark**:

- *Overview*: Skaters can visit the Ghent Skatepark, equipped with ramps and features suitable for skateboarders and BMX riders. It's a popular spot for those looking to showcase their skills.

Ghent Travel Guide 2024

GHENT

6. **Ghent University Sports Center**:

- *Overview*: Ghent University's Sports Center offers various facilities, including swimming pools, fitness areas, and sports halls. Visitors can participate in fitness classes, swimming, or other organized activities.

7. **Running in Citadel Park**:

- *Overview*: Citadel Park provides a scenic setting for jogging or running. The well-maintained paths and green surroundings offer a refreshing outdoor exercise option.

8. **Climbing at Biover Sport Blaarmeersen**:

- *Overview*: Biover Sport Blaarmeersen features a climbing wall for both beginners and experienced climbers. It's a great place to challenge yourself and enjoy indoor climbing activities.

9. **Fishing at Bourgoyen-Ossemeersen**:

- *Overview*: Bourgoyen-Ossemeersen nature reserve allows fishing in designated areas. Fishing enthusiasts can enjoy a peaceful experience surrounded by nature.

Ghent Travel Guide 2024

10. **Gentse Zesdaagse**:

- *Overview*: If you enjoy professional cycling events, check out Gentse Zesdaagse (Ghent Six Days). This annual track cycling race attracts international cyclists and offers an exciting atmosphere for spectators.

Whether you prefer a leisurely bike ride along the river, a round of golf, or an active day at the skatepark, Ghent provides a range of recreational options for all interests and activity levels.

CHAPTER NINE

Day Trips

Nearby Attractions and Excursions from Ghent

If you're looking to explore beyond Ghent, there are several nearby attractions and excursions that offer diverse experiences. Here are some places worth considering for day trips or short excursions:

1. **Bruges**:

- *Overview*: Known as the "Venice of the North," Bruges is a UNESCO World Heritage city with picturesque canals, medieval architecture, and cobblestone streets. Explore its historic center, visit the Belfry of Bruges, and indulge in Belgian chocolate.

2. **Antwerp**:

- *Overview*: Antwerp is a vibrant city known for its rich art history, including works by Flemish Baroque painter Peter Paul Rubens. Visit the

Cathedral of Our Lady, the Royal Museum of Fine Arts, and the trendy fashion district.

3. **Brussels**:

- *Overview*: Belgium's capital, Brussels, is known for its grand architecture, diverse neighborhoods, and iconic landmarks like the Atomium and Manneken Pis. Explore the historic Grand Place and savor Belgian waffles and chocolates.

4. **Mechelen**:

- *Overview*: Mechelen boasts a well-preserved medieval city center with attractions such as St. Rumbold's Cathedral and the Mechelen Toy Museum. Take a boat tour on the Dijle River or explore the city's cultural heritage.

5. **Ypres (Ieper)**:

- *Overview*: Ypres is a historic town with a poignant World War I history. Visit the Menin Gate Memorial and the In Flanders Fields Museum to learn about the region's wartime experiences.

GHENT

6. **The Ardennes**:

- *Overview*: The Ardennes region offers picturesque landscapes, dense forests, and charming villages. Outdoor enthusiasts can enjoy hiking, biking, and exploring the natural beauty of this serene area.

7. **Pairi Daiza**:

- *Overview*: Located near Brugelette, Pairi Daiza is a zoo and botanical garden known for its beautiful landscaping and diverse animal exhibits. It's a family-friendly destination with a focus on conservation.

8. **Kortrijk**:

- *Overview*: Kortrijk is a city with a mix of medieval and modern architecture. Explore the Broel Towers, visit the Kortrijk 1302 museum for medieval history, and enjoy the city's vibrant cultural scene.

9. **Gentse Hopper Boat**:

- *Overview*: Take a boat tour on the Gentse Hopper to explore the waterways around Ghent. This excursion provides a unique perspective of the city and its surrounding areas.

10. **Leuven**:

- *Overview*: Leuven is a university city with a lively atmosphere. Visit the historic University Library, stroll through the Old Market Square, and explore the city's botanical garden.

Whether you're interested in history, art, nature, or simply exploring charming Belgian towns, these nearby attractions and excursions offer a variety of experiences within easy reach of Ghent.

CHAPTER TEN

Practical Information

Currency, language, and useful phrases

Currency:

- The currency used in Belgium, including Ghent, is the Euro (€).

Language:

- The official languages of Belgium are Dutch, French, and German. In Ghent, Dutch is predominantly spoken. However, many people, especially in tourist areas, can communicate in English.

Useful Phrases:

1. *Hello*: Hallo

2. *Goodbye*: Tot ziens (formal), Dag (informal)

3. *Please*: Alsjeblieft (informal), Alstublieft (formal)

4. *Thank you*: Dank je (informal), Dank u (formal)

5. *Excuse me / Sorry*: Sorry / Excuseer (formal)

6. *Yes*: Ja

7. *No*: Nee

8. *Do you speak English?*: Spreekt u Engels? (formal), Spreek jij Engels? (informal)

9. *How much is this?*: Hoeveel kost dit?

10. *Where is the train station?*: Waar is het treinstation?

Remember, while many locals speak English, making an effort to use basic Dutch phrases is appreciated. Additionally, most signs and information for tourists are available in English.

Safety Tips

1. **Be Aware of Your Surroundings**:

- Stay vigilant and be aware of your surroundings, especially in crowded or unfamiliar areas.

2. **Secure Your Belongings**:

- Keep your belongings secure to prevent theft. Use anti-theft measures like money belts and secure bags.

3. Use Reliable Transportation:

- Opt for reputable transportation options and official taxi services. Be cautious with unofficial or unmarked vehicles.

4. Avoid Dark and Isolated Areas at Night:

- Avoid poorly lit or isolated areas, especially at night. Stick to well-traveled routes.

5. Stay Informed About Local Scams:

- Be aware of common scams and pickpocketing techniques. Stay informed about the latest travel advisories.

6. Emergency Contacts:

- Familiarize yourself with local emergency contacts, including:

  - **Emergency Services**: 112 (general emergency number)

  - **Police**: 101

  - **Medical Emergency / Ambulance**: 112

GHENT

7. **Health Precautions**:

- Carry necessary medications and know the location of nearby pharmacies. Familiarize yourself with local healthcare facilities.

8. **Stay Hydrated and Sunscreen**:

- If exploring during warmer months, stay hydrated and use sunscreen to protect against the sun.

9. **Follow Local Laws and Customs**:

- Familiarize yourself with local laws and customs to ensure a respectful and safe experience.

10. **Use Reputable Accommodations**:

- Choose reputable accommodations and follow their security guidelines. Use hotel safes for valuables.

11. **Emergency Evacuation Plan**:

- Be aware of emergency evacuation procedures at your accommodation and public places.

12. **Stay Connected**:

- Keep your phone charged and have a local SIM card or an international roaming plan for communication.

13. **Travel Insurance**:

- Consider travel insurance that covers medical emergencies, trip cancellations, and lost belongings.

14. **Local Emergency Services**:

- Identify the locations of the nearest police stations, hospitals, and embassies.

Remember that Ghent is generally a safe city, but it's essential to practice common-sense safety measures to ensure a secure and enjoyable visit. If you ever feel unsafe or encounter an emergency, don't hesitate to contact local authorities for assistance.

CHAPTER ELEVEN

Seasonal Guide

Best Times to Visit Ghent:

1. Spring (April to June):

- *Overview*: Spring is an excellent time to visit Ghent. The weather is mild, and the city comes to life with blooming flowers. Outdoor activities, festivals, and cultural events abound.

2. Summer (July to August):

- *Overview*: Summer brings warm temperatures, making it an ideal time for outdoor exploration. Ghent hosts various events, and the longer days allow for extended sightseeing. Be aware that it can be busy with tourists during this season.

3. Autumn (September to November):

- *Overview*: Fall is another favorable time to visit, with pleasant temperatures and fewer crowds compared to summer. The changing colors of the leaves add to the city's charm. Consider attending autumn festivals and cultural events.

4. **Winter (December to February)**:

- *Overview*: While winter brings colder temperatures, Ghent takes on a festive atmosphere during the holiday season. Christmas markets, decorations, and the Ghent Light Festival create a magical ambiance. It's a great time for a cozy visit if you enjoy winter festivities.

Considerations:

- **Tourist Seasons**: The peak tourist season is during the summer months (July and August), so if you prefer a quieter experience, consider visiting in spring or fall.

- **Weather**: Ghent experiences a temperate maritime climate. Summers are mild to warm, and winters are cool. Check the weather forecast and pack accordingly, especially if visiting in winter.

- **Festivals and Events**: Check the city's event calendar for festivals and special events that might coincide with your visit. Ghent hosts various cultural, music, and food festivals throughout the year.

Ultimately, the best time to visit Ghent depends on your preferences. Each season offers a unique experience, whether you're interested in outdoor activities, cultural events, or festive holiday atmospheres.

Festivals and Events throughout the Year:

1. Gentse Feesten (Ghent Festival) - July:

- *Overview*: One of Europe's largest cultural festivals, Gentse Feesten takes over the city with street performances, live music, theater, and a lively atmosphere. It usually lasts for ten days, transforming Ghent into a vibrant celebration.

2. Ghent Light Festival - February (biennial):

- *Overview*: The Ghent Light Festival is a biennial event that illuminates the city with captivating light installations. Artists from around the world contribute to the enchanting displays, creating a magical atmosphere.

3. International Film Festival of Ghent - October:

- *Overview*: This film festival showcases a diverse selection of international films, attracting filmmakers, actors, and cinema enthusiasts. It includes screenings, premieres, and discussions with industry professionals.

4. **Ghent Jazz Festival - July**:

- *Overview*: Jazz enthusiasts can enjoy the Ghent Jazz Festival, featuring performances by renowned international and local jazz artists. The festival takes place at various venues throughout the city.

5. **Flanders Festival Ghent - September**:

- *Overview*: Flanders Festival Ghent is a classical music festival that presents a rich program of orchestral and chamber music concerts. It attracts musicians and classical music lovers from around the world.

6. **10 Days Off - July (biennial)**:

- **Overview**: This electronic music festival takes place at Vooruit Arts Centre and various other venues. It features a diverse lineup of electronic and dance music artists, creating a dynamic atmosphere.

7. **Ghent Festival of Flanders - September to October**:

- *Overview*: The Festival of Flanders in Ghent celebrates classical and contemporary music with a series of concerts and performances. It showcases a range of musical genres and attracts both local and international talent.

8. **Red Bull Elektropedia Awards - November**:

- *Overview*: Recognizing achievements in the Belgian electronic music scene, the Red Bull Elektropedia Awards ceremony celebrates DJs, producers, and artists. The event includes live performances and honors various categories.

9. **Winter Festivities - December**:

- *Overview*: Ghent embraces the holiday season with winter festivities, including Christmas markets, festive decorations, and events. The city's squares and streets come alive with a festive ambiance.

10. **Belgium Beer Weekend - September**:

- *Overview*: While not specific to Ghent, the Belgium Beer Weekend in Brussels is a notable event for beer enthusiasts. It features a wide selection of Belgian beers, including tastings, beer-related activities, and celebrations.

These festivals and events add vibrancy and cultural richness to Ghent throughout the year. Whether you're interested in music, film, or the lively atmosphere of cultural celebrations, there's something for every taste and preference.

CHAPTER TWELVE

Photography Spots

Scenic Locations for Memorable Moments in Ghent:

1. Graslei and Korenlei:

- *Overview*: Capture the iconic view of medieval buildings along the Graslei and Korenlei canals. The picturesque setting is especially enchanting during sunrise and sunset.

2. St. Michael's Bridge:

- *Overview*:* St. Michael's Bridge offers a panoramic view of Ghent's skyline. It's a perfect spot to capture the cityscape, including historic buildings and the flowing river.

3. Castle of the Counts (Gravensteen):

- *Overview*: The Gravensteen, a medieval castle, provides a dramatic backdrop for photos. Explore the castle grounds and climb to the top for a unique vantage point of the city.

4. **Belfry of Ghent (Belfort)**:

- *Overview*: Climb the Belfry for breathtaking views of Ghent. Capture the city's rooftops and canals from this iconic medieval tower.

5. **Korenmarkt Square**:

- *Overview*: Korenmarkt Square is surrounded by stunning architecture. It's a lively area with historic buildings, outdoor cafes, and a vibrant atmosphere.

6. **Citadelpark**:

- *Overview*: Citadelpark is a serene green space with ponds, sculptures, and walking paths. It offers opportunities for capturing nature, including seasonal blooms.

7. **Vrijdagmarkt (Friday Market)**:

- *Overview*: Vrijdagmarkt, one of Ghent's oldest squares, is surrounded by historic buildings. The lively market square is ideal for capturing the city's dynamic atmosphere.

8. The Adoration of the Mystic Lamb (Ghent Altarpiece):

- *Overview*: Visit St. Bavo's Cathedral to see the famous Ghent Altarpiece. Capture the intricate details of this masterpiece by the Van Eyck brothers.

9. Ghent University Botanic Garden:

- *Overview*: Explore the Botanic Garden for a peaceful environment and beautiful flora. It's a hidden gem for capturing natural beauty within the city.

10. Waterside Views at Kraanlei and Coupure:

- *Overview*: Walk along Kraanlei and Coupure to capture charming waterside views. These areas offer a quieter ambiance and lovely reflections in the water.

11. The Three Towers of Ghent: St. Nicholas' Church, Belfry, St. Bavo's Cathedral:

- *Overview*: Frame all three iconic towers in one shot for a classic Ghent skyline photo. The combination of architectural styles is visually striking.

GHENT

12. **Canal Boat Tour:**

- *Overview*: Take a canal boat tour for a unique perspective of Ghent. Capture the city's landmarks from the water for memorable and distinctive photos.

Whether you're capturing the historic architecture, natural beauty, or vibrant city life, Ghent provides numerous scenic locations for creating lasting memories through photography.

CHAPTER THIRTEEN

Local Tips and Etiquette

Cultural Norms and Etiquette for Visitors

1. **Greetings**:

- *Norms*: Greetings are often accompanied by a handshake, and it's customary to use titles and last names in formal settings. In casual situations, a simple "Hallo" (Hello) suffices.

- *Etiquette*: Use a polite and friendly tone when greeting locals. If unsure, follow the lead of the person you are interacting with.

2. **Punctuality**:

- *Norms*: Punctuality is generally valued in business and social settings. Arriving a few minutes early is considered polite.

- *Etiquette*: Aim to be on time for appointments and social events to show respect for others' schedules.

3. **Dress Code**:

- *Norms*: Belgians typically dress neatly and conservatively. In more formal settings, business attire is appropriate.

- *Etiquette*: Dress modestly when visiting religious sites or attending formal events. Casual attire is acceptable in most other situations.

4. **Public Behavior**:

- *Norms*: Belgians value personal space and tend to be reserved in public. Loud conversations and public displays of affection are generally kept to a minimum.

- *Etiquette*: Be mindful of noise levels in public places and respect the personal space of others.

5. **Tipping**:

- *Norms*: Tipping is customary in restaurants, and it's common to round up the bill or leave a tip of around 10%. Tipping taxi drivers and hotel staff is also appreciated.

- *Etiquette*: Check if service charge is included in the bill. If not, leaving a small tip is a polite gesture.

6. **Language**:

- *Norms*: Dutch is the official language in Ghent. English is widely spoken, especially in tourist areas and among the younger population.

- *Etiquette*: Learning a few basic Dutch phrases can be appreciated, but most locals will be comfortable communicating in English.

7. **Dining Etiquette**:

- *Norms*: Wait to be seated in restaurants. Keep your hands on the table but not your elbows. Wait for the host to start the meal before eating.

- *Etiquette*: It's customary to say "Eet smakelijk" (Enjoy your meal) before starting to eat. Finish everything on your plate as wasting food is frowned upon.

8. **Respecting Local Customs**:

- *Norms*: Belgians take pride in their cultural heritage. Show respect for local customs, traditions, and historical sites.

- *Etiquette*: When entering religious sites, observe any dress codes and behave respectfully. Avoid interrupting ceremonies or services.

9. **Environmental Awareness**:

- *Norms*: Belgium places a strong emphasis on environmental conservation. Recycling is common, and there's an awareness of sustainability.

- *Etiquette*: Follow local recycling practices and be mindful of the environment. Avoid littering and dispose of waste responsibly.

10. **Queuing**:

- *Norms*: Belgians value orderly queues. Wait your turn in lines and avoid pushing or cutting in.

- *Etiquette*: Respect the queue system, whether in public transportation, museums, or other public spaces.

By embracing these cultural norms and etiquette, visitors can enhance their experience in Ghent and foster positive interactions with locals. Showing respect for local customs goes a long way in creating a memorable and enjoyable stay.

CONCLUSION

Your Ghent Adventure Awaits!

As we conclude this journey through the tapestry of Ghent, envision yourself as an explorer about to embark on a captivating adventure. Ghent, with its timeless charm and multifaceted allure, is not just a city to read about but an experience waiting to unfold.

Immersive Exploration:

Picture yourself navigating Ghent's cobblestone streets, discovering hidden gems and savoring local delights. The city's rich history, cultural treasures, and vibrant atmosphere are not just tales in this guide but promises of moments waiting to be lived.

A Warm Welcome Awaits:

From boutique hotels to the bustling neighborhoods, Ghent extends a warm welcome. The locals are ready to share their stories, the cuisine is eager to tantalize your taste buds, and every corner of the city is poised to reveal its unique charm.

Your Own Cultural Journey:

Imagine immersing yourself in the art and cultural richness, attending lively events, and experiencing the city's dynamic nightlife. Ghent isn't just a destination; it's an interactive canvas where you paint your own travel story.

Beyond Expectations:

As you explore beyond the city limits, imagine the anticipation of day trips to nearby wonders, adding depth to your Ghent adventure. The parks and gardens become your tranquil retreat, offering a moment of repose amid the vibrancy of the city.

Practical Wisdom for Seamless Travel:

Equipped with practical insights, you're ready to navigate Ghent with ease. The seasonal guide and photography spots offer glimpses into the city's ever-changing beauty, urging you to plan your visit with anticipation.

Local Insights for a Cultural Connection:

Finally, as you absorb the local tips and etiquette, envision yourself not just as a visitor but as a respectful guest, immersing yourself in the genuine warmth and authenticity that Ghent offers.

A Final Call to Adventure:

So, fellow traveler, as you close this guide, Ghent beckons you. It invites you to be more than a reader—it invites you to be an adventurer, a discoverer of its wonders. Your Ghent adventure awaits, and with every page turned, the anticipation builds.

Pack your bags, embrace the unknown, and let Ghent unravel its magic before you. The city is ready to welcome you, and the stories you'll create are waiting to be written.

Dank u wel for choosing Ghent. Your adventure begins now!

To serve you better, your honest feedback is highly appreciated.

With love from Betty Vanslyke

MY GHENT
JOURNAL

MyJournal

Title: _____   Date: _____

MyJournal

Title: _____   Date: _____

MyJournal

Title: _____ Date: _____

MyJournal

Title: _____   Date: _____

MyJournal

Title: _____   Date: _____

MyJournal

Title: _____   Date: _____

MyJournal

Title: ______________________ Date: __________

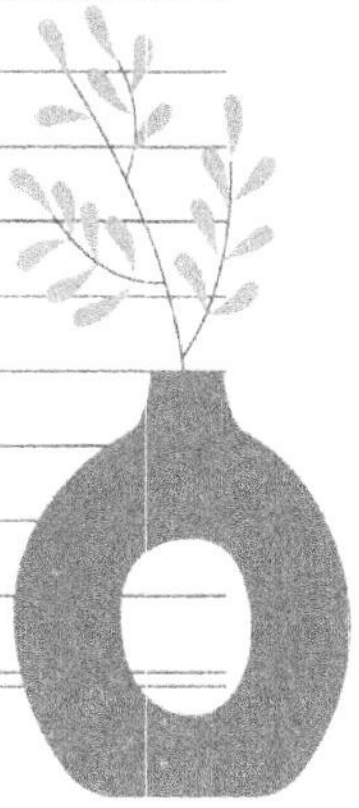

MyJournal

Title: _____ Date: _____

GHENT

MyJournal

Title: _____ Date: _____

MyJournal

Title: _____   Date: _____

MyJournal

Title: _____ Date: _____

MyJournal

Title: _____ Date: _____

#1 225000
#2 9822.

Printed in Great Britain
by Amazon